The Evergreens

A Play

David Campton

Samuel French–London
New York-Toronto-Hollywood

ISBN 0 573 12065 X

Please see page iv for further copyright information

CHARACTERS

Her In her late sixties. She has pretensions, aiming for a social status of which she is not quite certain

Him In his late sixties. He takes a mischievous delight in pricking Her pretensions. He is a little rougher in manner than Her and, realising how it irritates, makes himself out to be worse than he is, from time to time

Optional: Male and female Stage Manager(s)

The play is set in various locations and takes place in the late 1980s

SETTING

Although the staging is entirely up to the Director, properties could be mimed and the setting suggested by four chairs. These could be arranged to make a park bench, restaurant seating, a bus etc by Stage Hands dressed in black. With the addition of simple items of clothing - cap, scarf etc - these Stage Hands might even act as various non-speaking members of the cast: man on bench, waitress, Manager etc

David Campton

Other plays by David Campton published by Samuel French Ltd:

After Midnight, Before Dawn
Cagebirds
Can You Hear the Music?
Cards, Cups and Crystal Ball
Do-It-Yourself Frankenstein Outfit
Everybody's Friend
Life and Death of Almost Everybody
Mixed Doubles (with others)
Mrs Meadowsweet
Now and Then
Our Branch in Brussels
Parcel
Singing in the Wilderness
Smile
Us and Them
What Are You Doing Here?
Who Calls?
Winter of 1917
Zodiac

THE EVERGREENS

Him and Her entering arguing

Her The Queen! Why play the Queen?

Him If I'd known you had the King and the ace ...

Her Molly Perkins hadn't got the King or the ace. George Samson hadn't got the King or the ace. Who else could have had the King or the ace? The vicar, perhaps? Mrs Eldon-Pugh?

Him It was your King on my Queen.

Her Then Molly Perkins trumps my ace with a two of clubs. I've never seen playing like it. Over sixties? Under sevens could have played better.

Him I'd never have risked that third time. A child of two would never have risked a third time round.

Her A child of two would never have played that Queen.

Him A child of two shouldn't be playing whist.

Her Some people can't even play *Happy Families*.

Him I was asked to join the solo table.

Her You?

Him When I first joined The Evergreens. "Let me take you to the solo table," said Mrs Eldon-Pugh. "They're short of a good man at the solo table." "Thank you," I said. "I'm partial to a good game of solo." We started out for the solo table, and all of a sudden there you were - rising up amid the tea and biscuits.

Her "This is our latest member," said Mrs Eldon-Pugh.

Him And there you stood - blowing away the biscuit crumbs.

Fade in babble of voices in the background of The Evergreens Club

Her You! It *is* you - isn't it?

Him If you're you, I suppose I must be me.

Her You of all people. Here at St. Paul's Evergreen Club.

Him Small world, isn't it?

Her Thirty years, is it?

Him Gone - just like that.

Her It's a long time.

Him That's the way it goes.

Her Sit down.

Him I don't want to push in.

Her Oh, Percy won't mind moving over to the solo table, will
you, Percy? Just for this week. ... An obliging soul is Percy,
and nearly ninety. Oh, this is George Samson, and this is
Molly Perkins. We always play together. You're late, you
know. We start at half past two.

Him I went to the wrong place first. I got mixed up with the
expectant mothers.

Her Trust you. Just the same. Almost missed your tea. (*She calls
across the room*) Another cup of tea at this table, please. No,
Mary. Not seconds. A new member. ... Nice girl, Mary, but
just a bit officious. ... Oh, thank you, Mary. ... Marie biscuits
again, George. George doesn't like Marie biscuits. He always
gives his to me.

Him I like *any* biscuits.

Her (*disappointed*) Oh. That's all right then. Well, if we've all
finished tea, we may as well start again.

Him I haven't ...

Her You can finish your biscuit while you're playing. Don't
want to waste time, do we? After all, it's only a couple of hours
a week. ... Cut, George. Cut. ... Now it's your deal.

Him (*with a mouth full of biscuit*) Mine?

Her Clubs are trumps.

Him (*coughing on a crumb*) Well, then ... (*He deals*) Oh, I think
I may have put two down together there.

Her Trust you!

Him The cards are sticky.

Her Like the rest of us, they're getting on. Well, let's see what
you've given me. (*She tuts disapprovingly*)

Him (*gleefully*) Ah-ha. Ah-ha-ha-ha-ha-ha-ha.

Her You don't have to tell everybody what you've got.

*For the next few minutes they play. While she talks he tries to
concentrate on his cards. When she takes a trick she scoops it up
with a calm that does not quite conceal her glee. When a trick is*

lost she looks at him as though it were all his fault

Her Poor Gladys is away again. A couple of months ago she had
   half her inside taken away. We sent her a get-well card ... We
   ought to have taken that one ... There's Mr Comfrey. Very
   comfortable. Used to be an architect. All right then, Molly, an
   auctioneer if we must be pedantic. But very comfortable ...
   Ours ... Still drives. Usually picks up Miss Charles. Miss
   Charles is one of our older members. Her father was a Mr
   Charles. I forget exactly what he did, but it was talked about
   at the time.

A distant voice makes indistinct announcements

   There's really no need to hold an inquest on those cards.
Him Isn't somebody trying to tell us something?
Her Oh, don't worry. It's only Mrs Eldon-Pugh giving out the
   announcements.
Him She said "Annual Outing".
Her It's the same every year. Some want to go to the sea. Some
   want to go to the zoo. Some just want to drive around until tea-
   time. I'm sure I don't know why, when we can breathe petrol
   fumes any day without paying for the privilege ... Clubs *are*
   trumps, you know. ... Last year was a disaster. What did she
   say, Molly? Where are we going? ... Oh! We really are not
   concentrating, are we?
Him Can't win 'em all.
Her (*acidly*) You are so right. Mrs Eldon-Pugh is very sweet,
   and I don't know where we'd be without her. But she is a little
   overbearing at times. ... What are trumps?
Him She told me to come. "You want to join our Evergreens,"
   she said. "Drinking tea among the old 'uns?" I said. "It passes
   an afternoon," she said.
Her We're waiting.
Him For me? Oh.
Her If I were you, I'd never have played that Jack.

They get up, move one seat round the table, then play again

Him Just one afternoon a week. Funny how you get used to it.
Her If I were you, I'd never have played that spade.

They get up, move one seat round the table, then play again

Him Routine, like. I reckon if I missed a week now my boots'd
come on without me.
Her Who'd have thought that Mr Comfrey ... Miss Charles is
going to miss him. Mrs Eldon-Pugh sent a spray from The
Evergreens.
Him Marie biscuits again, George.
Her If I were you, I'd never have played that seven.

They get up, move one seat round the table, then play again

Him "I'm not old enough for an Evergreen," I told Mrs Eldon-
Pugh. "Who is?" she said.
Her If I were you I'd never have played that Queen.
Him (*throwing down his cards and standing*) Perhaps you'd like
to play my hand for me.
Her (*throwing down her cards and standing*) Oh, if you're going
to be petty ...
Him Petty?
Her If you don't want to be put right ...
Him If. If. If. If your aunt were your uncle, she'd wear trousers.
Her If you're going to be abusive ...
Him If. If. If. Damned silly word.
Her If I'd known ...

Fade Club background

Him If, if, if all the way. You take one trick now and lose the next
six.
Her If only one had known what one knows when there's no
longer any point in knowing.

*Fade in distant dance band music of the late forties. Him and Her
become younger, livelier*

Him If, if, if ...
Her All the way back.

Him If Bennet and Griggs hadn't just made that out-of-town offer ...

Her If Mildred Whitmore hadn't just hooked the Manager of the National Provincial ...

Him What young chap was going to turn down an offer like that?

Her Anything was possible thirty years back.

Him More like forty. Lads with Brylcreemed hair shining like their patent leather winkle-pickers. And all the girls trying to look like Veronica Lake.

Her It's a fox trot.

Him There'll be time for a fox trot later. I thought "There's always time."

Her I thought "There's all the time in the world when you're twenty".

Him Nearer thirty; but I thought "She's got a head on her shoulders".

Her "Encouragement," I thought. "A bit of encouragement and he will. But do I really want him to?" So - "I forgot my wrap" I said.

Him Shall I fetch it? ... "I could have been mistaken," I thought.

Her I thought, "Once he goes, I may lose him for good." So I said, "Distant music and moonlight on the rooftops: it's a pity to break the spell".

Him Aren't you feeling cold?

Her Not while we're close together.

Him I could put my arm round your shoulder.

Her I promise not to scream.

Him "Oh-ho," I thought, "I could go a lot further than that and she'd not scream." But I said, "Comfy?"

Her "Mmmm." ... But I thought, "Those buttons on his sleeve are digging into my shoulder".

Him I thought, "This is how they set a fractured collar-bone". But I said, "Ah".

Her What could I say to that? So I said nothing, but nestled my cheek against his shoulder.

Him I thought, "Powder, all over my best suit".

Her I thought, "He's bound to say something soon".

Him "Should I tell her about the promotion?" I thought. "Nothing like a Bank Manager's pay, but the right sort of wife could push a man on," I told myself. "But a wrong 'un's like a millstone," I answered back. And I looked at her sideways, appraising.

Her "What is he rolling his eyes at?" I thought. "Is there a wild streak in him I've missed?" ... But I said, "You're very pensive tonight".

Him I think you ought to know ...

Her "He's steady, reliable, and better than nothing at all," I thought. "But if Mildred Whitmore could marry into the National Provincial Bank, what might not be possible? There'll be other balconies and other boys. When there's a chance of caviare, why settle for hot-pot? What if next week ...? But he's going to ask now, so I'll have to answer now. Yes or no?" ... So I said, "I love that tune."

Him I thought, "She's not bad-looking and it's not all painted on. But can she cook?"

Her "They'll say 'Congratulations'", I thought. "But what if they mean - she could have done better than that?"

Him I thought, "My arm's gone to sleep". And I said "Ooooh!"

Her What's the matter?

Him My shoulder. Just a twinge.

Her Does it often take you like that?

Him It's the unaccustomed exercise.

Her Let me rub it for you.

Him You?

Her I'm good with shoulders.

He gives a yelp

There.

Him (*beginning to enjoy the massage*) Ah!

Her Better?

Him You've got the touch.

Her You were going to say something.

Him Was I?
Her It couldn't have been very important.
Him I'm going away soon. New job. Out of town.
Her Oh, yes?
Him It's a step up.
Her Congratulations.
Him Thanks.

The distant band is now playing "Auld Lang Syne"

Her Isn't that *Auld Lang Syne*?
Him I thought we'd got more time.
Her There's still time.

The dance music fades

Her All the time in the world.

Fade in Evergreens Club background

Him (*coming out of the dream*) What did you say?
Her Roll on next week.
Him (*conciliatory*) Let me help you on with your coat.
Her (*relenting*) I hope you came in *your* coat.
Him Wrap up, I say. Aren't you wearing a scarf?
Her My gloves are in my pocket.
Him So are mine. But I brought a scarf, too.
Her (*disapprovingly*) City colours?
Him Prevention is worth all your hot lemon and aspirin.
Her You're never going out without a hat.
Him There's my balaclava to go on first.
Her Is that absolutely necessary?
Him Never give the cold a chance to strike.
Her It's not the cold. It's the waiting.

*Fade Evergreens background. Fade in street with traffic. A bus
passes*

Him Was that your bus?
Her It never is.
Him And when they do come, they're full of youngsters.

Her In my young days we were made to stand.

Him The Chinese are brought up to respect the old.

Her We're not old.

Him We're not Chinese, either.

Her Did you go to China?

Him When?

Her You said your job took you out of town.

Him That job took me all over the place. Manchester. Bradford.
       Leeds. Sheffield. Bolton...

Her But not China.

Him We didn't have a branch in China.

Her You didn't write. Not in all those years. Not once.

Him You didn't write, either.

Her I didn't know where you were.

Him This is your bus. Stick your hand out.

A bus passes

Her Full.

Him Youngsters.

Her Why don't they walk? I was taught to walk. I'd walk now,
       only it's silly to walk home when there's a bus.

Him I've been thinking.

Her When it stops.

Him Don't you think it's silly - just meeting at The Evergreens?
       After all, there's more to a week than Tuesday afternoons.
       We've all the time in the world, yet we see no more of each
       other than we do of George Samson and Molly Perkins. We
       were friends.

Her Not just good friends. Very good friends.

Him So - I thought you might come round to my place some
       time.

Her That's very kind.

Him Being friends.

Her It might be better if you came to my place, though. Being
       on the bus route.

Him We could meet at your place one time, and my place

another time.

Her That would be nice.

Him We'll meet at my place first.

Her I did suggest my place.

Him I suggested my place first.

Her But then I suggested my place.

Him We're not going to quarrel over the place, are we?

Her Of course not.

Him Tomorrow, then.

Her About six?

Him That's settled. I'll see you tomorrow. At six. At .... Hey, this *is* your bus. And it's stopping.

A bus draws up, slightly distant

Her Half way up the road as usual.

She exits

Him Hey - driver. Wait. We're not training for the Olympics.

Her (*off*) Tomorrow.

Him At six.

The bus drives off

He encounters something against his knees. He looks down

Him Whoops. Hey, sonny, look where you're going. Want to know the time? Or do you want helping across the road? .... You want to help *me* across the road. Do I look as though I - ? Oh, very well. I was in the Cubs myself. Not so long ago. This can be both our good deeds for the day.

He exits

Fade in clock chiming six

She enters on one side of the stage

Her (*talking to a budgerigar*) Joey. Joey. There's a pretty boy. It's all ready on a tray, you see. Crisps and tomatoes and potted meat sandwiches. I'll sit in this chair here, and he'll sit in that chair there. Won't that be cosy? I'll hand the sandwiches to him. Or he'll hand the sandwiches to me. Whichever is handy. And we'll talk. Of this and that. He can be quite charming, Joey. When he tries. And I think this evening he'll try. Eh, Joey? Eh?

Time signal pips are heard from a radio followed by a muffled news reader speaking

> *He enters on the other side of the stage*

Him She'll be here any minute. (*He switches the radio off*)

A dog woofs

> Mind out of the way, dog. You'd like to get your teeth into this. When did you last see a cold cut of of beef like that, girl? Something to slice at there. Though I don't mind telling you we'll be living on porridge oats for the rest of the month. And there's pickles. And beet. And horseradish. A few spring onions would have rounded it off. But spring onions, when consumed by only one of the parties, can prove to be proper passion killers. Now I wonder if...

Her I wonder if a whisper of parsley over the sandwiches would look tempting. Better not. It may confuse him. He wouldn't know whether to eat it, leave it or stick it in his buttonhole. That sort of speculation can dry up conversation completely. And this evening we are going to talk, Joey. Once I've opened ..... Oh, there, now: I forgot to bring it out. Silly me.

> *She exits*

The dog woofs

Him It's the kitchen for you tonight, girl. Until we find out how she feels about dogs. The really big question is - do I bring out the surprise as a surprise or would it be more surprising to have it ready - casual like? - "It so happens I have a bottle open." Yes, that strikes the right cosmopolitan touch.

> *He exits*

She returns

Her There, Joey. A bottle of brown ale. He likes his glass of
brown ale. So useful to remember these things.

He returns

Him British Cream Sherry. What will she say to that? Wagging
your tail, are you? Let's hope she wags her tail, too. She'll be
here any minute. Any minute now.

Her He should be here any minute now, Joey. Though it might
appear more hospitable if he found the bottle open when he
arrived. There's something mean-looking about an unopened
bottle or an uncut pie. As though they were never meant to be
started on. That was his bus going by. He should be on it.
Better be quick with the bottle opener.

She goes out

Him I wonder this is the right stuff. She used to be fond of sweet
things. Better try a drop to make sure. (*He pours wine and
tastes*) Yuck! She's going to love that. Now I'll have to wash
the glass again. Don't want her to think I started without her.

As He goes out, She returns

Her He couldn't have been on that bus after all, Joey. I expect
he'll be on the next one. Should a bottle of beer lose many
bubbles in ten minutes? It only goes to show that one should
never be over-eager.

She breaks off as there is a distant flap at the letter box

Someone at the door! He must have been on that bus after all.

As She goes out, He returns

Him At least she didn't catch me wiping the glasses. Any
minute now, girl.

The dog woofs

Don't worry, girl. I shan't put you in the kitchen until she's actually at the door.

She returns

Her Fancy people pushing things through letter boxes at this time of day. "Boy Scouts' Rummage Sale." That's not the way to attract rummage, I can tell you. Stop worrying, Joey. If he said he'll come, he'll come. We'll just sit here quietly and wait for him.

Him Make yourself comfortable, girl, while we wait.

Her Just wait.

Him And wait.

Her And wait.

The Lights fade slightly. The clock strikes seven

Seven o'clock.

Fade in "The Archers" signature tune, which is switched off

Him Don't tell me. I know what time it is.

Her Of course he'll be all apologies when he does come.

Him Act as though nothing had happened.

Her Think nothing of it. I'll say. What's an hour between friends.

Him Is it really that time? I'll say. I hadn't noticed. (*Pause*) If I'd known she was going to be as late as this, I wouldn't have cut the bread so soon.

Her I wonder if I can find a cork for the bottle. Yes, Joey, a cork for the bottle.

Him Down, girl. Don't you get restless, too.

Her Time hasn't changed him.

Him Women! I've put up with 'em often enough in my lifetime. The times I've been left standing about.

Her His convenience is all that matters. I suppose he stopped for a drink with the boys.

Him Let her be late if she likes. After all, girl, we sit alone every other night. What's another hour or more?

The clock strikes the half hour

She's not coming, is she?

Her He's not coming. He never meant to, did he?

Him If she meant "no", why did she say "yes"?

Her Why say "yes" in the first place? Thought he was being funny I suppose.

Him Her idea of putting me in my place, I suppose. Vindictive.

Her Uncouth yobbo! No, not you, Joey.

Him Silly bitch! No, not you, girl.

Her If he thinks we can still be friends after this, he's got another think coming.

Him As far as I am concerned, we are no longer on speaking terms.

Her And when we do meet again...

Him I'll tell her so.

Her There goes another bus. But I won't peep round the curtain to see if he's coming.

Him I won't wait.

Her He won't be coming anyway. Well, we don't care, do we, Joey? We didn't make dainty sandwiches just for him, did we? We like dainty sandwiches.

Him I suppose she thinks I sit down to a cold beef supper like this every night. Well, let her.

Her I'm only sorry now I didn't sprinkle the sandwiches with parsley. The test of a conscientious cook - does she sprinkle her potted meat sandwiches with parsley when there's nobody to see them?

Him If only I'd known, I'd have had spring onions.

Her They're beginning to curl.

Him I've a good mind to set to right now - horseradish, beetroot, pickles, the lot.

Her That's the trouble with dainty sandwiches. They soon curl.

Him Only, somehow, I don't feel like it.

Her But he did say he'd come, Joey. He did.

Him At least I shan't have to shut you in the kitchen, old girl. Better take this lot back there instead.

He exits

Her "Rummage Sale. Saturday. Please give generously." I wonder if the Boy Scouts could use a bottle of flat brown ale...

She exits

The lights go down and up

She enters with hat and coat

Yes, Joey. We're going to the park this morning. We're going to watch the people going by. If one sits in the park for long enough, there's no telling who one may see. Of course there are certain persons one would rather not see, but that is a risk one must take when one sits on a bench in the park.

She exits

Fade in park background

He enters and comes up to a park bench.

Him There's nobody else sitting here, is there, lad? I mean, you weren't saving the seat for anybody, were you? You don't mind if I sit next to you, then. (*He unfolds a large newspaper*). This paper's a bit awkward to fold. I'm not used to the *Financial Times*. I usually take the *Mirror*, but the boy left the wrong paper this morning. The *Financial Times* costs more than the *Mirror* so it would have been a pity to pass up a bargain. Even if it is more difficult to fold. I'm not disturbing you, am I, lad? These benches were made to hold four, you know. Or two and the *Financial Times* ...I - er - see you've got the *Mirror*. You weren't by any chance expecting the *Financial Times*?...I just thought I'd ask. Because it would have been odd if you'd been sitting there with my *Mirror* and while I was sitting here with your *Financial Times*. .... Oh, I'm not suggesting that you have got my *Mirror*, lad. Oh, no. I'm just saying that the chap who'd got my *Mirror* is the last person I'd expect to find sitting next to me. As indeed it wasn't. That's what I mean by coincidence. Coincidence is when two people you would never expect to find together...Actually - find themselves...Together.

She enters and comes up to the bench

Her Excuse me, young man. Is this end of the seat unoccupied?
... Thank you. I only ask because all the other places appear to
have been taken. The park is unusually full this morning.

Him Some people think they own the place.

Her One realises that in a public park one has no option but to put
up with whoever one finds oneself sharing a bench with.

Him Some people have a funny idea of their own importance.

Her Some people ought to be ashamed of themselves.

Him Some people ought to be banned.

Her Some people ought to wash out their mouths with soap and
water.

Him Some people ought not to make nuisances of themselves.

Her Some people ought to be reported to the Park Keeper. ....Oh!

Him Hey, I didn't mean...Why should that young chap suddenly
get up and walk away?

Her What I was saying had nothing to do with him.

Him Perhaps he thought it had.

Her Well, if the cap fits...

Him (*looking at his paper*) I see gilts are down again. ....You may
be wondering why I am reading the *Financial Times*.

Her No.

Him Oh? Have it your own way.

A slight pause

Her Why?

Him Ah. You want to know now, do you?

Her No.

Him Please yourself.

A slight pause

As a matter of fact, I am reading the *Financial Times* because
I thought you might ask me.

Her Ask you what?

Him Why I'm reading the *Financial Times*.

Her You can read what you like.

Him Thank you.

A slight pause

It's easy enough to talk to strangers. Any old words will do.
When it's somebody you know, you have to find the right
opening. And the right words aren't so easy to come by.
Especially when you're not on speaking terms.

Her Why *are* you reading the *Financial Times*?

Him I'm glad you asked me that.

Her Why?

Him Because now we're talking again.

Her Life is too short to bear grudges.

Him Doesn't bear thinking about.

Her And, after all, you did apologise.

Him Apologise?

Her Not as gracefully as you might have done thirty years ago.
But I don't suppose you skate as gracefully as you did then,
either.

Him I never...

Her And we are friends.

Him Have been for forty years now. We may not have seen each
other for thirty years, but we never had a cross word in all that
time.

Her One needs friends. Now more than ever. The world isn't
what it used to be.

Him It's the only one we've got.

Her To say nothing of the cost of living.

Him Doesn't leave much out of a pension. Only a few pennies
in your pocket.

Her And you're likely to be hit on the head and robbed of *them*.

Him The police aren't what they used to be. Even when you can
find one.

Her In too much of a hurry.

Him Like all the other youngsters.

Her Youngsters have no respect.

Him Pushing and shoving and screaming and dressing like something out of the ark.

Her Out of the jungle.

Him There's a pair now behind the rhododendrons. No, don't look. It'll only upset you.

Her What are they doing?

Him I don't know. But if they have to go behind the rhododendrons, I bet they shouldn't be doing it.

Her I blame the parents.

Him And the teachers.

Her And the magistrates.

Him They don't care.

Her They're too young.

Him I think they've done behind the rhododendrons.

Her Not before time.

Him I could complain. Get it stopped.

Her You might complain, but you won't get it stopped. There aren't enough of us. We ought to stick together. It's us against the permissive society.

Him The permissive society won't lose any sleep over that. There they go.

Her Aren't they both boys?

Him Can't believe your eyes these days.

Her (*briskly changing the subject*) Time for lunch. Did you bring your sandwiches?

Him No. As a matter of fact...

Her Well, as we're together .... You don't mind if I join you?

Him Where?

Her Oh, haven't you decided? There's a little place by the gate. Very reasonable.

Him I suppose ...

Her Personally I never have more than a cup of coffee and a lettuce leaf at this time of day.

Him In that case ...

Her That couple from behind the rhododendrons - they're coming back.

Him Come on - let 'em have the bench.

They exit

Fade park background. Fade in Café background

They enter

Her It isn't The Grand Hotel, of course. But what is, these days? Not even The Grand Hotel. And I do like a tablecloth. What's the matter with you?

Him (*twitching his shoulders*) My braces.

Her I wouldn't know anything about braces. Would a safety pin be of any help?

Him You've got a safety pin?

Her Some of us learn by experience.

Him You're a godsend.

Her You're welcome.

Him (*calling*) Oh, Miss ... Miss..... Where's the - ? No, not the menu. Oh, yes. I see...

He hurries off

Her (*to the waitress*) I can't see anything to laugh at, girl. you're new here, aren't you? ..... They usually are. Either they leave to better themselves, or they don't improve and are sacked.... But the tablecloths are clean. Usually. One feels that someone, somewhere is trying. ..... No need to flutter your pad, girl. I'll order when my friend comes back. No wonder Chinese takeaways are cropping up all over the place.

He returns jauntily

Him Oh, that's a relief.

Her You ought to learn how to sew.

Him It's all very well for a woman. If she loses her knickers, she can always step out of 'em.

Her Really! The waitress doesn't want to know that. She is waiting for your order.

Him What are you having?

Her A cheese salad. You couldn't do better yourself.

Him At these prices I want to feel my moneysworth going down.

What's the cheapest? Something with chips. Eggs and chips then. Does bread and butter come with it?

Her *(watching the waitress go)* Giggle, giggle, giggle. At what?

Him I call a spade a spade.

Her I wasn't talking about spades.

Him Braces, then. Safety pins. Knickers.

Her My, my. We are enjoying ourselves, aren't we?

Him They're words, that's all. Describing everyday objects.

Her It's so easy to let oneself go.

Him What do you mean - let myself go?

Her I only mention the subject because I'm sure you hadn't noticed. This streak of coarseness must have crept up on you unawares. I won't say any more. If you want to think any more about it - that's up to you.

Him Oh - safety pins. *(He yelps)* Oh bloody safety pin!

Her You're wearing that joke out.

Him Must have come undone. It's digging into my spine. Ah! Must do something about it. Oh. Oh, Oh....

He lurches out

She gives way to laughter, which she stifles almost immediately

Her Yes? The cheese salad is for me. The chips are for my friend. He won't be long. Thank you. I'm sure he won't mind my starting. After all, it must be provoking to see someone enjoying a cool salad when one has to munch one's way through a pile of chips. Salads are good for you. I wonder if I shall ever persuade him.

He returns

Him That won't come undone again in a hurry.

Her Don't let your chips get cold. I hope you didn't mind my starting on the salad.

Him I never touch lettuce away from home. After all, you never know what may be lurking in the undergrowth.

Her Poor Mr Comfrey was fond of his chips. He went out like a light..

Him There's only one thing worse than finding a caterpillar and that's finding half a caterpillar.

Her They do say his arteries were completely clogged.

Him Greenfly's a different hazard. It takes a good scrubbing to get rid of your greenfly. These people haven't got the time.

Her Every chip another nail in his coffin.

Him Salad cream's the only answer. If you can't get rid of 'em any other way, smother 'em

Her Not that I'm trying to influence you. Eat what you like.

Him Have a chip.

Her But I know how men cater for themselves. Beer, bread and fish and chips....

Him Go on. Have one.

Her Most unhealthy.

Him It's one thing to be virtuous. It's another to go hungry. Help yourself.

Her Well.... If you can spare it.

Him That's right. Have another.

Her If I do, it's to prevent you from eating it.

Him Don't worry about that. Here. Have these.

Her Not so many.

Him I'm going to order another lot. Hey, miss. Hey. Oh ... (*He breaks off with a slight cry*)

Her Trouble with your trousers again? I'm sure the management could supply you with a piece of string.

He gives a slight moan

I'd offer to sew on your buttons if you didn't think I was intruding. Good intentions can so easily be misinterpreted. Tongues wagging like pendulums. If I make a suggestion, it's only because I have your best interests at heart. After all, we are friends, and if friends can't make suggestions, then who can? A word in the right place at the right time. That's all. Between friends. If the safety pin is such an embarrassment to you, why don't you....

He moans

Why ...? *Is* it the pin? .... Are you all right?

He moans

Help! Oh. Miss .... Miss! I think my friend ... Fetch the Manager.

He moans

There, there. Don't worry. I'm with you. It's heart. Like Mr Comfrey. It was the chips. Don't touch those chips, I warned him. ... Give him air. Doesn't anybody know what to do 'till the ambulance comes? Don't crowd so. Go back to your tables. If only he'd stuck to the salad. Even if it was crawling with caterpillar and swarming with greenfly, it would have been better than those deadly chips. ... What? Then the other customers shouldn't have been listening. You can't move a dying man. ..... No, of course you're not. Just a figure of speech. We're going to lay you out in the Manager's office. I mean.... Can you find your feet?

She supports Him off

As soon as He is out of sight she rapidly returns to the table

He hasn't touched that roll and butter. Waste not, want not.

Deftly she sweeps it into her handbag

She leaves defiantly

Fade Café background

She assists Him back. He is wearing an enveloping dressing gown

Her We can sit in this chair for a few minutes while our bed is made.

Him Whose bed?

Her Your bed.

Him Then say so. It's not *our* bottle of pills, it's *my* bottle of pills. It's not *our* dicky ticker, it's *my* dicky ticker. It's not *our* funeral, it's *my* funeral.

Her It's nobody's funeral. The doctor is very pleased with us.

Him I don't know what you've been doing for him.

Her We're a bit fractious today, aren't we? Sure sign we're getting better. But we musn't tire ourselves before beddybyes, must we?

Him Why is it a sick-room reduces any woman to gibbering lunacy?

Her We didn't say that about our nurse in hospital, did we? Sledgehammer Sarah we called her.

Him She wasn't a woman, anyhow. She was a steam-driven machine.

Her I'm glad we appreciate these little differences. Time for supper. Ah, that brightens you up, doesn't it?

Him What delicious confection have you whipped up for me tonight?

Her Arrowroot.

Him Oh, God!

Her Light and nourishing, so that we can slip straight off to sleep.

Him If I get any thinner, I'm going to slip straight down the loo. For safety now, I have to hang on to the chain.

Her My father had a regular bowl of arrowroot until the night he died.

Him A merciful release.

Her Such a patient man.

Him He'd need to be.

Her I shan't be long.

She exits

Him For arrowroot I can wait. (*Some of his following remarks are shouted, others are muttered to himself*) I thought I could smell onions. Why did you let me smell onions while you were mashing that mess?

Her (*off*) I was scrubbing out the stewpot.

Him Stew! With onions and shin and suet dumplings .... I could shift a plate of stew now. With potatoes and carrots and peas and thick, brown gravy. And you go on mixing arrowroot! Can't you put an onion in it?

Her (*off*) Ugh!

Him Give it some flavour anyway. Forget the arrowroot. Get me bread, cheese and half a pint.

She returns

Her And have you writhing before morning? Let me tuck a serviette into your pyjamas.

Him I'll tuck in whatever has to be tucked in.

Her As you wish. Tuck into this like a good boy. I'll read while you enjoy your supper.

Him Slop!

Her (*reading from the newspaper*) "Brown, Cedric. Seventy two, Lockett Avenue. Suddenly at home. From sister Carrie. All enquiries to the Co-operative Society Funeral Service.

Him That's the despatches!

Her I always turn first to the Births, Deaths and Marriages. Don't you?

Him Only to make sure I'm not among 'em.

Her These days I seldom recognise names among the births and marriages.

Him Did you know Cedric Brown?

Her No. Did you?

Him Then it doesn't really matter, does it?

Her It matters to him.

Him Not now. (*Stirring his gruel*) Round and round the garden...

Her You won't find any lumps in that arrowroot.

Him A lump might vary the monotony.

Her "Elkington, Sarah. Twenty two, Kissinger Street ... Oh, that's not even local. Farr, Stanley aged one hundred and forty. I think that must be a misprint. Gray, Dolly."

Him Goodbye, Dolly Gray.

Her Really!

Him You've got to laugh. You can't sit there, watching the cemetery fill up, and ask to be serious.

Her If you'd rather I turned to the horoscope....

Him No. Carry on. Don't want to miss an old friend on the way out.

Her Hope, Anthony, of "The Cedars"...... He was the magistrate.

Him Referred to a Higher Court.

Her That' s exactly what it says here. Not what I should have written, but .... There's more than one entry for him. Six, seven, eight, nine ... Rather wasteful when one considers the cost.

Him Perhaps they want to make sure he won't come back after an appeal.

Her "Thomas, Mildred. Eighteen, Huntingdon Walk. Sleep well, Grandma, from Arnold, Cissie, Iris, Mabel, Bert, Ethel, Vera, John, Maureen, Dottie, Horace, David, Coral, June, Ivor, Mervyn, Stephen, Pat and all at forty four, Bassington Street. A rest well earned."

Him No comment.

Her If you've finished with that bowl, I'll take it away.

Him Why?

Her You don't want to drop it.

Him I mean - why?

Her Oh - that. Actually it's all part of the undertaking service. They're very helpful.

Him You mean the boys in black are in cahoots with the local rag?

Her At a time like that one is glad to have someone who will shoulder the responsibility.

Him And stick it on the bill. It's not as if it does any good - except to the lads who are on to a good thing. It doesn't mean anything.

Her It means one is leaving behind someone who is sorry to see one go.

Him Then for once I'm lucky. I shan't be leaving anybody.

Her One can't always be sure about that.

She exits

Him I don't want it. None of your black overcoats and professional long faces. None of your snuffling services in draughty chapels. None of your flowers left to wilt on the clay. Just shovel me in quick and get it over with.

She returns

Her Is that a general observation or a precise instruction?

Him I said nobody's going to miss me, and I mean nobody's going to miss me.

Her That's not entirely up to you, is it? ... Where are your socks?

Him I don't ask anybody to miss me.

Her I may as well find something for my fingers to do while I'm waiting.

Him Anyway, I'm not gone yet. .... Waiting?

Her Bed at half past.

Him I've always darned my own socks.

Her So I see. With a hole this size, how did you know which end to put your foot in?

Him Independent. "I can manage," I told 'em at the hospital. "I don't need your District Nurses and your Home Help". I've always been independent.

Her That's what you told them.

Him I didn't ask for women swarming all over the house.

Her "The duty that lies nearest," my father used to say. He was most appreciative of what was done for him.

Him They try to make out a man can't stand on his own. "Independent?" they say. "Why, you can't even darn your own socks".

Her "Don't think it isn't appreciated", he would say. "Because it is." He was rather old fashioned with those little courtesies. Of course, I'd have done exactly the same if he hadn't said a word. What else was there to do? He said nobody could mix arrowroot the way I did.

Him They're on the watch for that moment of weakness.

Her Of course, nobody ever did.

Him A dizzy spell, a tightness in the chest and they've got you.

It's arrowroot and bed at half past after that. If you're not careful, they'll even write your obituary for you. "Why did he have to go?" they write. If you could answer back, you'd say "It was the only way out of their clutches". But you can't answer back then. Safer to stay independent.

He waits for a reply, but none comes

I'm independent.

Still no reply

Did I ask anybody to make my bed for me? Did I ask anybody to mix messes? I've always been independent. When I can't do for myself, they can wheel me away for good. Nothing personal, you understand. It was good arrowroot - if you've a taste for baby food. But it's so easy for a man to lose his independence. And when it's gone, it's gone. All he can do after that is be appreciative.

Her I thought we were friends.

Him I'm an independent man.

Her Aren't we friends?

Him I'm still independent.

Her I'll - finish the other socks later. One can so easily strain the eyes.

Him So easy to sell your birthright for a mess of arrowroot.

Her Even if we hadn't been friends, I'd have done what I could. The duty that lies nearest becomes a habit. Though between friends it's not always easy to distinguish between duty and pleasure. Perhaps it's a pity the human race had to be made up exclusively of men and women. If I'd done as much for Molly Perkins, there'd have been no misinterpretation of a natural gesture. I did what I could, that's all. I'm sorry if .... I didn't intend to ... But I thought that, being friends, you would understand. (*She sniffs*)

Him I said we're friends, didn't I?

She says nothing but takes a deep breath

Oh, hell! I didn't mean to ... I was making a general observation.

Nothing personal. Trust a woman to take a general observation personally.

She sniffs again

I'm not blaming anybody. After all, there's no harm in friends doing things for friends .... All right then. I'm sorry I spoke. I mean... I can't stand people crying all over the place.

Her I wasn't going to cry.

Him That's all right, then. (*He struggles with himself to say something comforting, but cannot find the words*) I mean ... Oh, hell!

Her It doesn't matter.

Him It does.

Her I understand perfectly.

Him No, you didn't. I'm trying to say...

Her There's no need to.

Him You're not making this any easier.

Her Sorry.

Him There you go again.

She sighs

Him I was about to say ... (*He waits for an interruption which does not come*) As long as we understand each other...

Her We're friends.

Him Good friends.

Her Just good friends.

Him I think it's time I went to bed.

Her I put a hot water bottle in it.

Him I can find my own way.

Her Naturally.

Him Drop the catch on the front door when you go out.

Her I always do.

Him Evergreens tomorrow?

Her Soon be time for the Annual Outing.

Him Annual Outing, eh?

Her You know what that will be like. A four hour traffic jam going. Four hours in a shelter on the Marine Parade. A fish tea and a four hour traffic jam on the way back. Mrs Eldon-Pugh believes the Annual Outing should appeal to the lowest common denominator.

Him I'll be there. Tell them they won't find me among the despatches yet.

Her I'll tell Mrs Eldon-Pugh you'll be on the bus.

Him And - er - Well - er ... That is - er ... Thank you.

Her You're welcome.

He goes out one way, She another

Bus background with chattering passengers

He sits on one side of the gangway, She on the other

Her As usual.

Him Didn't you expect it?

Her Four hours on a grotty bus and two in a freezing shelter.

Him It faced the sea.

Her And reeked of stale shrimps.

Him I paddled.

Her You've got a hole in your sock.

Him Tea wasn't bad.

Her There was a fly in the milk. And you did nothing about it.

Him What did you expect me to do - throw it a life-belt?

Her You could have complained.

Him Why didn't you?

Her It's a man's function to complain.

Him You've got a funny idea of a man's functions.

Her Crude as ever.

Distantly other Evergreens on the bus begin to sing "Side by Side"

Him They've started singing already.

Her Mrs Eldon-Pugh is taking up a collection for the driver.

Him They're hoping he'll pull up for a drink half way back.

Her Don't expect me to put anything in the hat for that.

Him It wasn't a bad day out, really.

Her Same as all the others.

Him We sat like this last year. You on one side of the gangway and me on the other.

Her Your fault for being late.

Him This time next year we'll still be sitting like this.

Her Do you think so?

Him With that lot singing their heads off, making believe they're happy.

Her A lot can happen in a year.

Him There'll still be an Evergreens, though.

Her I suppose so.

He puts out his hand. She sees it, but pretends not to notice. He knows that She has noticed and continues to look ahead with his hand held out. Without looking at him She takes his hand, even though this involves a certain amount of trial and error. They hold hands across the width of the bus gangway. After a while He begins to sing. After a while She joins in. Until they end the chorus together

CURTAIN

FURNITURE AND PROPERTY LIST

Please see the author's note on page v. A list of essential properties is given below for use where these are not mimed

Playing cards
Biscuits
Coat and gloves (**Him**)
Coat and gloves (**Her**)
Scarf (**Him**)
Budgerigar in cage
Food (**Him**)
Food (**Her**)
Hat (**Her**)
Financial Times (**Him**)
Safety pin (**Her**)
Bread roll
Dressing gown (**Him**)
Serviette
Bowl of arrowroot
Newspaper

LIGHTING PLOT

Various interior and exterior settings
No fittings required

To open : Interior lighting

Cue 1	**Her:** " ... any point in knowing." *Lighting change*	(Page 4)
Cue 2	**Her:** " ... all the time in the world." *Lighting change*	(Page 7)
Cue 3	**Her:** "It's the waiting." *Lighting change*	(Page 7)
Cue 4	**He** exits *Lighting change*	(Page 9)
Cue 5	**Her:** "And wait." *Lights fade slightly*	(Page 12)
Cue 6	**She** exits *Lighting change*	(Page 14)
Cue 7	**She** exits *Lighting change*	(Page 14)
Cue 8	**They** exit *Lighting change*	(Page 18)
Cue 9	**She** leaves defiantly *Lighting change*	(Page 21)
Cue 10	**He** goes one way. She another *Lighting change*	(Page 28)

EFFECTS PLOT

Cue 1   **Him:** " ... away the biscuit crumbs."   (Page 1)
Babble of voices in Club

Cue 2   **Her:** " ... talked about at the time."   (Page 3)
Indistinct announcement

Cue 3   **Her:** " ... If I'd known ..."   (Page 4)
Fade Club background

Cue 4   **Her:** " ... any point in knowing ..."   (Page 4)
Fade in dance band music

Cue 5   **Her:** "Congratulations."   (Page 7)
Band plays "Auld Lang Syne"

Cue 6   **Her:** "There's still time."   (Page 7)
Dance music fade. Fade in Club background

Cue 7   **Her:** "It's the waiting."   (Page 7)
Fade Club. Fade up street and bus passing

Cue 8   **Him:** "Stick your hand out."   (Page 8)
Bus passes

Cue 9   **Him:** "And it's stopping."   (Page 9)
Bus draws up

Cue 10   **Him:** "... at six."   (Page 9)
Bus drives off

Cue 11   When ready   (Page 9)
Fade in clock striking six